FAQ
TEEN LIFE™

FREQUENTLY ASKED QUESTIONS ABOUT

Juvenile Detention

Corona
Brezina

ROSEN
PUBLISHING®

New York

Published in 2012 by The Rosen Publishing Group, Inc.
29 East 21st Street, New York, NY 10010

First Edition

Library of Congress Cataloging-in-Publication Data

Brezina, Corona.
Frequently asked questions about juvenile detention/Corona
Brezina.—1st ed.
      p. cm.—(FAQ, teen life)
Includes bibliographical references and index.
ISBN 978-1-4488-5560-5 (library binding)
1. Juvenile detention—United States—Juvenile literature.
2. Juvenile detention homes—Law and legislation—United
States—Juvenile literature. 3. Juvenile justice, Administration
of—United States—Juvenile literature. I. Title.
KF9825.B74 2012
365'.420973—dc22

                                                        2011013702

Manufactured in China

CPSIA Compliance Information: Batch #W12YA: For further information, contact Rosen Publishing, New York, New
York, at 1-800-237-9932.

Contents

WHAT DOES IT MEAN TO BE "IN THE SYSTEM"?

The juvenile justice system is made up of courts and agencies that deal with the crimes and wrongdoings of young offenders. Teenagers who commit a wrongdoing answer to probation officers, judges, and other legal figures when they face the consequences of their actions. "The system," for these young people, is the jurisdiction of the juvenile court. Teenagers involved in the system will quickly learn their legal rights and obligations as the court decides the details of their penalty. There are millions of children and teenagers "in the system" in the United States.

The philosophy and practices of juvenile justice in the United States have tended to shift throughout the years. In the nineteenth century, children were treated with the same penalties as adults under the law. Beginning in the early twentieth century, authorities began to deal with young offenders separately, viewing the court's function as a more parental role. This trend changed from the 1960s onward, after a landmark Supreme Court case found that juvenile offenders were entitled to basic constitutional rights that were denied in the juvenile court system. During the 1970s and 1980s, many Americans were disturbed by apparent increases in the amount and severity of juvenile crime. There were objections that the juvenile justice system was too lenient and that young offenders should pay for their crimes. Many juvenile courts began issuing harsher penalties.

In 2005, the Supreme Court handed down a landmark ruling (*Roper v. Simmons*) that offenders could not be executed for crimes committed under the age of eighteen. The ramifications of the ruling raised new debates about the juvenile justice system. In the opinion, the Court stated that juveniles were fundamentally different from adults. They lacked adult maturity and sense of responsibility. They were more susceptible to influences such as peer pressure. Their personalities were not yet fully formed. Because of this "diminished culpability," the Court decided against imposing the death penalty on a juvenile for a crime that would merit the death penalty for an adult. After the ruling, later studies of juvenile justice programs found that intervention and rehabilitation, rather than punishment, were more effective for young offenders, especially those who had committed lesser crimes.

The juvenile justice system is separate from the criminal justice system that deals with adults. The criminal justice system is interested primarily in punishment and deterrence of crime. The juvenile justice system, though it has evolved from its roots, still presents itself as a parental stand-in. It holds that young offend-

A juvenile court judge addresses a youth charged with delinquency. The judge carefully considers the child's specific needs in handing down the penalty.

ers can be rehabilitated. Proceedings are less formal and adversarial than in criminal court trials. Judges are allowed more discretion in their rulings. Offenders are likelier to receive less restrictive penalties.

The term "juvenile detention" is commonly used as a synonym for the incarceration (imprisonment) of juvenile offenders. In the legal system, however, it has a more specific meaning. Juveniles are *detained* immediately after being arrested. Juvenile detention, therefore, is the period of temporary custody before a court appearance. After the trial, the judge may rule that the offender be *committed* to a correctional facility. Two common terms for incarceration are "residential placement" and "juvenile institution." Older terms, less used today, include "juvenile hall" and "reform school."

A Fragmented System

There is no national juvenile justice system in the United States. Each state has its own set of laws and procedures for dealing with juvenile offenders. In some states, a police officer can legally interrogate a minor without a parent or lawyer being present. Juvenile offenders are indeed entitled to their Miranda rights, but they don't always understand the consequences of waiving their rights, which can lead to them being interrogated without their parents' knowledge or legal counsel. (The rights contained in the Miranda warning ["You have the right to remain silent. If you give up the right to remain silent, anything you say can and will be used against you in a court of law. You have the right to an attorney. If you desire an attorney and cannot afford one, an attorney will be obtained for you before police questioning."], called Miranda rights, were established in a groundbreaking U.S. Supreme Court case, *Miranda v. Arizona*, in 1966. In that case, the Court ruled that statements made by someone accused of a crime could not be used as evidence against that person in a trial unless the accused voluntarily waived the constitutional right to remain silent.)

Some states allow bail for young offenders; others do not. After being arrested, a child can wait from one to three days for a detention hearing depending on state law. (At the detention hearing, the judge will decide whether or not the offender will be held in custody before trial.) Some states, but not others, will appoint a lawyer to represent the child. Types of treatment programs, and eligibility for programs, also vary from state to state.

Different states define "juvenile" with different age ranges. In most states, young people under the age of eighteen are dealt with in the juvenile justice system. In some states, though, the upper limit is seventeen, or even sixteen, years old. Some states also define an age of responsibility. Children under this age— ranging from six to ten—are considered too young to understand the consequences of their actions.

Even the definition of punishable offenses varies from state to state. Differences are particularly pronounced in dealing with status offenses—behavior that is illegal solely because of the offender's age. Examples include truancy, possession of alcohol, running away, and curfew violations. States vary on how they categorize status offenses and in the penalties dealt out to violators.

The structure of the juvenile justice system is also variable. Some states have a centralized system under state control. In others, services—including detention facilities and institutions— are run at a local level or some combination of state and local control. Large cities, for example, may run juvenile justice services independently of the state system.

Hearings generally take place in juvenile court, but in some states, it is called family court or probate court. In some states, the juvenile court is a division of the criminal court system; in

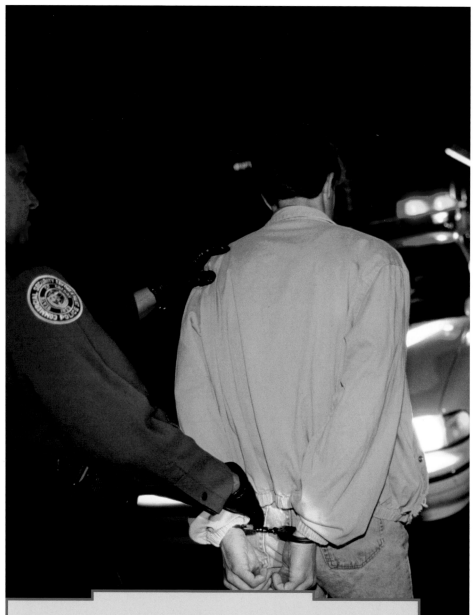

A police officer takes a young man into custody. Some legal experts advise that juveniles who are under arrest should refuse to give a statement unless there is an attorney present.

others, there is a specialized juvenile court. Some states have separate juvenile courts for different types of cases, such as serious delinquency, minor delinquency, and family matters like custody disputes. Navigating the juvenile justice system can be a daunting prospect, and the lack of coordination between states and even within states makes a difficult situation even more challenging.

Juvenile Justice by the Numbers

Nationwide, statistics relating to juvenile justice are tracked by the U.S. Department of Justice (DOJ). In 2007—the most recent year with data available—juvenile courts handled about 1.67 million juvenile delinquency cases. (This number does not include status offenses.) That totals about 4,600 cases every day. From 1960 to 1997, delinquency rates steadily increased. Since 1997, total numbers of delinquency cases in courts have declined by 11 percent. Most of this drop is due to a steep decrease of 30 percent in property crimes, which include burglary, larceny, theft, and arson.

Despite the decline, property offenses still accounted for the largest number of juvenile offenses—594,900 cases, or 36 percent of all cases. Next were public order offenses, which include crimes such as weapons offenses, nonviolent sex offenses, and disorderly conduct. This accounted for 472,300 cases, or 28 percent of the total. Personal offenses—including crimes such as homicide, forcible rape, robbery, and assault—made up 25 percent, or 409,200 cases. The remaining 11 percent—190,100 cases—were drug crimes.

A juvenile offender on probation talks to his probation officer, who monitors teen offenders attending his high school. Probation, not residential placement, is the most common penalty for young offenders.

Status offenders are not considered "delinquent" in legal ter-minology. In 2007, the juvenile court system formally dealt with 150,700 cases of status offenses. The court often handles status offenses informally, and the penalty in these cases is likely to be lighter.

Seventy-nine percent of the offenders under juvenile court jurisdiction were between the ages of ten and fifteen, the remaining 21 percent being sixteen or seventeen. The numbers of sixteen- and seventeen-year-old offenders are actually higher than the statistics indicate because they are tried as adults in some states. Male offenders significantly outnumbered female—73 percent of offenders were male. White offenders accounted for 64 percent of all cases, black offenders for 33 percent, and Asian and American Indian cases for 1 percent each.

Out-of-Home Placement

The obvious question asked by a juvenile offender, new to the system or not, is, "Are they going to lock me up?" The answer depends on the individual case, but statistics offer an overview of the types of offenses that are likely to carry serious penalties, such as residential placement.

Some younger offenders are detained in custody before going before a judge. In 2007, 364,600 offenders spent time in detention—slightly more than one out of five.

Not all juvenile offenders go before a judge in formal proceedings. In the cases that were heard formally, the offenders were "adjudicated delinquent," or found guilty, 63 percent of the time. The most frequent disposition was probation, accounting for 56 percent of all sanctions. Nineteen percent received some other sanction, such as a fine, counseling, or community service.

The remaining 25 percent adjudicated delinquent received a disposition of out-of-home placement. This accounted for 148,600 cases—fewer than one out of ten of all total offenders. Thirty-three percent of the offenders given an out-of-home placement disposition were property crime offenders. Public order offenders made up 29 percent of the total. Public order offenses include crimes such as escaping from institutions and parole and probation violations. This inclusion may explain why the figure is proportionately so high—judges are likely to be tougher on repeat offenders.

Status offense cases are very unlikely to result in out-of-home placement, with only 9,700 status offenders given the penalty. Truancy was the offense most likely to receive a disposition of out-of-home placement.

In 2006, there were about ninety-two thousand juvenile offenders being held in residential facilities. Just six states—California, Florida, New York, Ohio, Pennsylvania, and Texas—accounted for nearly forty-four thousand offenders. This number does not reflect rates of incarceration, however, since all of these states have large populations. Colorado, Florida, North Dakota, South Dakota, and Wyoming had the highest rates of offenders being held in residential facilities. Hawaii, Maryland, Mississippi, New Jersey, and Vermont had the lowest.

Myths and Facts

If the police take a teenager into custody, he or she will probably be confined to a juvenile detention facility. Fact: ➥ The primary objective of the juvenile justice system is rehabilitation, not punishment, and juvenile court officials aim to impose the least restrictive sentence that is adequate to the offender's needs. Many offenders are not even required to go before a judge. For offenders who do receive a formal hearing, only the most serious and chronic offenders are likely to be confined to a residential facility.

Juvenile crime rates have been escalating in recent years. Fact: ➥ The number of delinquency cases in the juvenile justice system peaked at 1997 and has gradually dropped since then. Arrest rates and the number of offenders committed to residential facilities follow similar trends. Juvenile crime is a serious issue, but crime rates are not increasing; they are actually going down.

Myth A juvenile court record is automatically erased when the offender turns eighteen, whether the offender was placed in detention or not.

Fact: ➡ In most states, a person must file an expungement motion with the court in order to clear a juvenile record. This is very important—even if a juvenile was taken into custody just once with no charges filed, it still could show up, for example, during a background check for a job. Certain serious crimes may not be eligible for expungement. Some government background checks will uncover a juvenile record, even if it has been expunged.

two

HOW ARE TEENS SENTENCED TO JUVENILE DETENTION?

The juvenile justice system is intended primarily to rehabilitate young offenders. Whenever possible, the judge and other officials prefer to pursue lighter penalties than placement in a detention facility. Residential placement disrupts an adolescent's life at a critical point in his or his development. The teenager is suddenly ripped away from family, friends, work, and school. Any student who has missed school for a few days because of sickness or a vacation knows how tough it is to catch up afterward. Returning to normal life after an extended period of incarceration is many, many times more difficult.

There are other considerations besides the offender's welfare. Studies have shown that confinement, especially in facilities similar to adult jails, does not help reduce recidivism, or committing further crimes after being released. Nor does it reduce crime rates in the community. A high rate of juvenile confinement in a state tends to bring public concern that the system is not taking adequate prevention and intervention measures regarding juvenile crime. In addition, it is very expensive to hold an offender in a residential facility. According to the Justice Policy Institute, the cost amounts to about $240 per day.

Referral and Intake

Most young offenders enter the juvenile justice system when they are brought in by the police. Some are reported by parents, school officials, probation officers, or victims of crimes, but more than four out of five (according to the DOJ) are referred by the police. Being stopped by the police does not automatically lead to involvement in the juvenile justice system. Police officers have the discretion to let a suspected offender off with a warning. They may, after talking to the teenager and his or her parents, issue a citation without pursuing further legal penalties.

In legal terminology, adults are arrested but juvenile offenders are "taken into custody." Juveniles do not have all of the same legal rights as adults, though laws vary from state to state. Police do not always need a warrant to arrest a juvenile, for example, and juveniles can be taken into custody for status offenses.

After being referred to the juvenile justice system, the offender proceeds to the intake department. The intake officer consults with the offender, his or her parents, and the victim, if appropriate. The officer also reviews the offender's personal his-

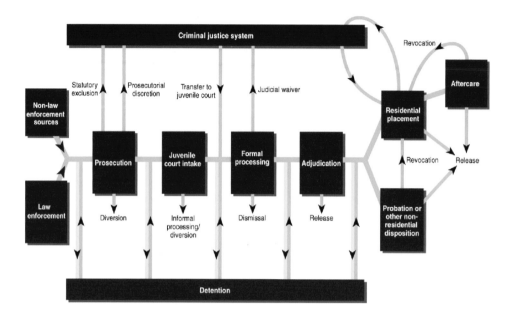

This diagram depicts the possible stages for a case going through the juvenile justice system. The offender enters the system at the left, when brought in by law enforcement or non-law enforcement sources.

tory and juvenile record, if he or she has one. At this point, the intake officer may decide to dismiss the case. Otherwise, the officer recommends either that the case be handled informally or else heard formally in a courtroom at an adjudication hearing— the juvenile justice equivalent of a criminal trial.

Many nonviolent cases are likely to be eligible for informal handling (also called diversion), especially when the teenager is a first-time offender. The offender must admit to being guilty of the crime and agree to the terms of diversion. Diversion requirements are usually light—typically informal probation, community service, or counseling. Cases handled informally do not receive a severe penalty such as placement in a detention facility. The offender can avoid establishing a court record. If the offender violates probation or commits a subsequent crime, he or she may be referred back to intake or be required to attend an adjudication hearing.

Judicial Waivers

After intake, some offenders are transferred to adult criminal court through a waiver. A prosecutor or a judge may decide to initiate the transfer. In some states, a certain number of offenses committed by a certain age will trigger a mandatory waiver. The juveniles transferred to adult court are considered the most serious, chronic, and violent offenders. Each state sets the minimum age that juveniles can be transferred for a certain offense, usually between fourteen and sixteen, but it can be as low as ten years old.

The number of juveniles transferred to adult criminal court spiked during the 1990s, and the practice has proven controversial. Young offenders are much likelier to receive harsh sentences in adult court. They are much more likely to be arrested again after leaving prison than offenders in the juvenile justice system. In addition, young criminal offenders are held in adult prison with adults once they are convicted. There, they are either housed with adult convicts, where there is a high potential for abuse, or held in isolation, which can be psychologically damaging.

Young people awaiting adjudication in Sacramento County Juvenile Hall in California may be held in this new dormitory-style unit, a space that provides security but very little privacy.

Juvenile Detention

If the offender is instead scheduled for an adjudication hearing, the court then decides whether he or she should be held in detention until the hearing. A juvenile offender can legally be held in detention for a short period of time after being taken into custody—usually for twenty-four to seventy-two hours. The court determines in a detention hearing whether the offender should remain in detention or be released. A detention hearing, presided over by a judge or other detention hearing officer, is less formal than a trial. Detention is likely in cases of serious crimes when there is probable cause that the offender committed the crime. It is also likely to be recommended if there are special considerations, such as a history of failing to show up for court proceedings. In 2007, according to the DOJ, about 22 percent of delinquency cases involved detention. The detention rate for status offenders was 9 percent.

Conditions inside detention centers vary greatly. Facilities house anywhere from a couple dozen to hundreds of offenders. Some have strictly enforced regulations, while others are more relaxed. Schedules typically include mealtimes, schooling, recreation, and other activities such as group discussions.

There has been much criticism of detention procedures. It is a short-term, temporary arrangement. Therefore, there is little in the way of relevant educational or treatment programs, but the interval is still long enough to disrupt the teenager's life. It can be a traumatic disruption because many facilities are overcrowded and understaffed. Studies have shown that detention was a factor in increasing recidivism—young people who had been detained were more likely to commit subsequent crimes. A stint in detention has also been shown to negatively affect mental health, especially for teenagers already in need of mental health services.

Over half of the youth in detention centers are held for nonviolent crimes. Critics argue that they do not qualify as high-risk offenders and it would be better for the teenagers, their communities, and the juvenile justice system if the overall rate of detention were reduced.

Alternatives to Juvenile Detention

A formal adjudication hearing is similar to a criminal trial, with prosecution and defense lawyers making their cases before a judge. There is generally no jury in juvenile court. Both sides may call witnesses, introduce evidence, and cross-examine witnesses. At the end of the hearing, the case is dismissed or the juvenile is adjudicated delinquent—found guilty. The disposition, or sentence, is handed down at a separate disposition hearing. Before the hearing, a probation officer compiles a disposition report including the offender's juvenile record, personal history, family circumstances, and other relevant information. The disposition report also recommends a sanction. The judge consults the disposition report before delivering the disposition. Ideally, the disposition is the least restrictive sanction that is required to achieve the court's objectives for the offender.

Most offenders do not receive a disposition of residential placement. The most commonly handed-down disposition is probation. Over half of all offenders are given probation.

Offenders on probation are allowed to return home and go to school, but they are subject to certain restrictions. Probation is a very flexible penalty. A probation officer monitors the offender to ensure that he or she does not violate the terms of probation.

Certain conditions are standard for offenders on probation. An offender must not commit further crimes or associate with anyone with a criminal background. He or she may not leave the area without permission. Drug testing may be required. Other conditions may be more intensive and depend on the individual

A St. Paul, Minnesota, social worker meets with teens participating in a diversion program that gives troubled youth the opportunity to perform community service as an alternative to incarceration.

case. The offender may be required to complete a drug treatment program, pay restitution for damages, or earn a high school degree. An alternative to traditional probation is school-based probation, in which a probation officer works inside a school. The officer has more regular contact with offenders and is able to easily monitor academic progress and behavior at school.

Some dispositions let offenders return home without formally placing them on probation but impose certain sanctions. An offender may be required to perform community service, pay a fine, or pay restitution. Unlike a fine, restitution goes to the victim of an offense—such as property damage—as compensation. Sometimes the court requires that an offender be confined to home during certain hours or monitored with an electronic device. Both of these conditions restrict the offender's movements to some degree. Offenders are often required to undergo counseling—anger management, drug counseling, family counseling, therapy, or some other form. Some juvenile justice systems provide drug courts or gun courts, which are intervention programs intended to change offenders' behavior. Serious offenders may be sent to day treatment programs, which generally combine correctional treatment services and education.

In some cases, the judge may not want to send the offender home but does not think the offender needs to be placed in a residential facility. An offender may be placed in foster care, a group home, or a halfway house. These facilities generally provide treatment and support in a nonsecure setting, meaning that the offenders will not be locked in or confined.

WHAT ARE THE DIFFERENT TYPES OF JUVENILE DETENTION FACILITIES?

Types of juvenile residential facilities vary widely. Young offenders are most likely to be committed to a large "training school," similar to an adult prison that houses between one hundred and five hundred inmates. Other facilities may resemble private homes or school campuses. There are varying levels of security from one institution to another. Facilities may be public or private. Private facilities are not equivalent to private schools; it just means that the state awards a contract to a privately run institution instead of operating it publicly with state employees. These are usually smaller than government-run facilities.

The different types of institutions have different goals for the residents. The most serious offenders are kept in prisonlike maximum-security facilities to reduce their

A resident of a young women's detention facility browses through a book. Some states offer gender-specific programs designed to meet the needs of female juvenile offenders.

opportunities to commit further crimes. They are considered a danger to the community. Most institutions focus on rehabilitation as well as deterrence.

By law, however, juvenile offenders cannot be housed alongside adults in jail. A 1974 law required "sight and sound separation" between juvenile offenders and adult criminals. Compliance with the law was slow, partly because of limited facilities. In addition, some states consider sixteen- and seventeen-year-olds to be adults. Young offenders waived to adult court are treated as adults by the court and may be sent to adult jail and prison.

Offenders are generally separated by gender—large state-run training schools serve either males or females. Female offenders make up a small proportion of offenders in detention facilities. In 2006, only 15 percent of offenders being held were female. Some critics have argued that because there are relatively few females in detention facilities, the juvenile justice system neglects to address their specific needs.

Short-Term Detention

As described earlier, detention is generally intended as a temporary stretch of time before formal adjudication. There are other transition points at which offenders may be held in detention, however. Offenders may return to detention while waiting to be transferred to a residential facility. After being released from a residential facility, the offender may be placed in detention before returning home. If the offender cannot return home after being released, he or she may have to remain in detention while alternate housing arrangements are determined.

Detention facilities have many functions, and critics claim that this is a factor in the facilities being overused and over-crowded. They say that many of the teenagers in detention do not need to be locked up and that they are held for too long.

Some states have specialized short-term facilities for post-adjudication offenders. An offender may be sent to a reception center or diagnostic facility for evaluation. Many offenders have

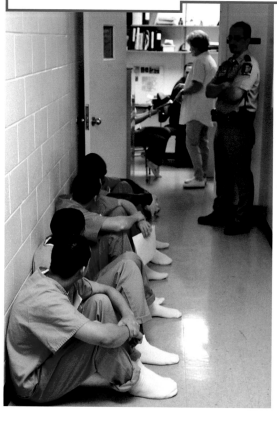

Juvenile offenders wait to receive psychological testing and evaluation at a Texas evaluation center. They will then be transferred to other facilities to complete their sentences.

problems with mental illness or substance abuse, sometimes severe. If necessary, they will undergo a variety of medical and psychological evaluations. Social workers also review offenders' family history and background. These factors will all help determine a final rehabilitation plan. In states without specialized diagnostic centers, offenders may be evaluated in private facilities or on-site at residential facilities.

Young offenders, especially nondelinquent youths, may spend time in youth shelters during transitions from one stage of treatment to another. Shelter care facilities primarily provide housing to status offenders as well as dependent and neglected children—nonoffenders whose parents cannot care for them. Youth shelters are usually unlocked, though residents have limited freedom to come and go without permission. Conditions in youth shelters vary, but many are small facilities that emphasize a homelike environment.

Training Schools

More young offenders are sent to large training schools than any other type of residential placement. Terms for these facilities vary from state to state—they may have names such as youth center or juvenile residential facility. They are the most secure placement for young offenders, who are often locked in their rooms behind locked main doors behind locked razor-wire fences. When there is public debate over "juvenile prisons" or "juvenile correctional institutions," these are the types of facilities under discussion.

Some training schools hold a range of offenders, while others focus on a specific group. In addition to different levels of security, training schools may focus on addressing specific needs. A maximum-security institution may emphasize its safe and secure environment. A medium-security facility may present itself as a therapeutic community for girls.

Offenders in training schools are strictly supervised. Many of the residents are considered potential threats to facility staff and other inmates. They are not allowed to possess anything that could be used as a weapon. In some cases, this means that inmates cannot even keep books in their rooms. Furniture is often bolted to the floor. Staff members monitor residents as they move from one area to another, and in the most secure facilities, inmates wear restraints between rooms. Strict regulations cover every aspect of daily life, from mealtimes to showering.

A training school may consist of a single building or a campus-style layout. Residents typically live in small rooms, sometimes with a roommate, in larger units of twenty-five rooms or so.

Residential Treatment Facilities

The most common type of facility, by the numbers, is the residential treatment facility. Residential treatment facilities generally house fewer offenders than training schools. They are more likely to be privately run.

Residential treatment facilities provide services to offenders with mental illness and substance abuse problems. These offenders have generally received a disposition of an out-of-home placement from a judge, but their offenses are not serious enough for them to be sent to a training school. Facilities might be "staff secure," meaning that offenders are monitored by staff rather than locked in. Residential treatment facilities generally offer twenty-four-hour care.

There is no standard legal description of a residential treatment facility, which makes it difficult to compare different programs for effectiveness. They employ a variety of treatment methods, such as therapy, counseling, and medication. Many residents are academically challenged and receive special education services. Critics of residential treatment facilities suggest that more research needs to be done on addressing young people's psychological and substance abuse problems so that such programs can take a more focused approach. Nonetheless, some surveys have shown that residential treatment programs have positive effects on participants.

Residential treatment facilities can overlap in categorization with boot camps, wilderness camps, and group homes of various types. All of these programs may offer treatment programs combined with their different approaches toward rehabilitating young offenders.

Alternative Approaches to Residential Placement

Juvenile boot camps became popular during the 1980s and 1990s as an alternative to traditional training schools. The philosophy behind boot camps is that a disciplined environment will have a positive long-term effect on attitudes and behavior. Although practices vary from one boot camp to another, they all tend to emphasize military-style routines. Residents—often called cadets or recruits—spend long days involved in often physically demanding activity and abide by strict regulations. They may live in dormitories modeled after army barracks. Staff members take on the role of military instructors. Cadets in boot camps are mainly nonviolent or first-time offenders, and boot camps primarily target male offenders.

Studies have produced mixed reviews of the effectiveness of boot camps. Residents' behavior does improve during their stay in boot camp. The programs fail, however, to reduce recidivism, one of the chief goals. Recidivism rates proved nearly as high in boot camps as in traditional residential facilities. Boot camps have also proven controversial due to allegations of harsh treatment of residents. There have been instances of participants dying during boot camp.

A captain at an Illinois boot camp shows a group of new arrivals how to order meals (for instance, raising two fingers means that the inmate would like two portions). Talking in line is not permitted.

Another approach takes juvenile offenders out of institutions altogether. Juvenile forestry camps (also called wilderness camps) and ranches present offenders with challenging outdoor activities. Unlike boot camps, which stress strict discipline, these programs emphasize building self-confidence. Residents in wilderness camp receive training in basic outdoors skills. Throughout their stay, they may periodically undertake outdoors expeditions such as hiking, canoeing, and rock climbing. Wilderness camps serve offenders at a variety of levels—most participants are low- or medium-level offenders, but some camps do target serious and violent offenders. Youth ranches place offenders in a rural setting, where they spend much of their time outdoors, sometimes doing conservation projects or working with animals.

Group Homes

Group homes are another placement option for young offenders, especially offenders who do not require a secure detention setting. They also serve nonoffenders who require a more secure placement than foster care. Group homes, which are often located in residential neighborhoods, generally house between five and fifteen offenders. Staff members live in the homes and try to create a structured and supportive family-style atmosphere. Group homes also take a therapeutic or treatment approach. In general, residents can leave the home for school and some other approved activities.

Group homes have not been proven to reduce the recidivism rate significantly for residents relative to other forms of placement. In addition, neighbors often object to a group home being located in the community.

Halfway houses are similar to group homes in that they are generally staff secure and situated in a community setting. Slightly larger than group homes, they are intended to support offenders who are making a transition out of secure residential placement or substance abuse treatment programs.

WHAT IS IT LIKE IN JUVENILE DETENTION?

Any teenager facing a period in residential placement is bound to wonder—and dread—what sort of ordeal awaits. At worst, descriptions of juvenile detention sound like horror stories. At best, the process successfully rehabilitates the offender. Institutions generally try to make offenders comfortable, but the experience is not designed for enjoyment.

Ideally, a judge hands down a disposition based on a careful analysis of the teenager's needs. A supportive parent is in attendance and has given input helpful toward developing a rehabilitation plan. The probation officer has closely documented factors relevant to the case. If the teenager's lawyer believes that the disposition is too harsh, he or she argues the point and suggests an alternate strategy. The result is a rehabilitation plan carefully tailored to the individual teenager. It addresses both the behavior and any

As part of the Ounce of Prevention Services (OOPS) program, juvenile offenders learn about what they might expect to experience if they were sentenced to residential placement.

root causes of the behavior, such as mental illness, family conflict, difficulties at school, gang involvement, or substance abuse. The offender is placed in a program that best matches his or her needs.

In reality, however, not every case receives such careful scrutiny. Judges and probation officers are often overworked with huge caseloads. Not all judges have training and experience specific to the juvenile justice system. Many offenders lack adequate counsel when going before the judge. On every level, the juvenile justice system is hobbled by scarce resources. In addition, there are high rates of substance abuse and mental illness among juvenile offenders. These problems can cause difficulty and anguish even for teenagers supported by their families in stable homes. It is even more difficult for juvenile justice facilities to address the complicated personal needs of every troubled young person in the system. The result is a strained system and, in some cases, inadequate residential facilities.

Length of Stay

After being taken into police custody, any teenager's reasonable thought is, "When am I going to get out of here?" Minor first-time offenders are often released to their parents and may avoid any formal involvement in the system. For offenders headed to residential placement, the process is much longer. Shortly after being taken into custody—three days or less—the offender attends a detention hearing. The average stay for offenders sent to detention is fifteen days. The next step is the adjudication hearing and, if the case is not dismissed, the disposition hearing. The disposition hearing may occur directly after the adjudication or at some later date. A longer delay could mean that the teenager may spend another couple weeks in detention. After receiving the disposition, the offender may have to wait still longer in detention before being transported to the residential facility.

In adult criminal court, where the objective is punishment, an offender is given a specific length sentence. In juvenile court, where the objective is rehabilitation, dispositions are more likely to be indeterminate in length—the teen will remain incarcerated until deemed rehabilitated. If the offender does not successfully complete a treatment program, for example, his or her participation may be extended.

Average lengths of stay vary greatly from one program to another and from one state to another. Residential training

Juvenile offenders enrolled in the VisionQuest wilderness program march during a celebration marking the opening of the African American Civil War Memorial in Washington, D.C.

schools have the longest lengths of stays, in the range of eight to twelve months. Programs at wilderness camps vary widely in length; a typical stay may last six to nine months. One of the best-known programs, VisionQuest, runs for twelve to fifteen months. Boot camp programs tend to be shorter, in the range of four to six months.

Family Contact

Visitor policies vary from one institution to another. In general, offenders in residential placement facilities may receive visits from parents and close family. There are generally specific visiting hours, and institutions—especially training schools—often have strict guidelines for visitors. Visitors will probably have to show a photo ID and may be required to pass through a metal detector.

Offenders are generally allowed to make phone calls to their parents and other family members with some restrictions, such as time limits or weekly number of calls. Visiting and telephone privileges might depend on the offender's security status and behavior. An offender may earn greater visiting and phone privileges as a result of good behavior. Institutions generally allow residents to send and receive letters. Some facilities allow occasional visits home, such as for a weekend or holiday, especially when the offender has been making good progress.

Residential facilities are often located in isolated areas far from the residents' homes. The long distance can make it inconvenient for parents to visit their child. This may be particularly difficult for poor families that might have trouble paying transportation expenses, especially if a parent has to take time off from work to arrive for official visiting hours.

Daily Activities

All residential facilities provide educational services, counseling and mental health programs, and recreation activities. The particular focus depends on the program. Most institutions recognize that it is important to provide a well-balanced variety of services that address a broad range of needs.

Teens work with small engines in a vocational class at the Illinois Youth Center in Joliet. The facility is considered an Illinois model for change due to its success in rehabilitating serious offenders.

Educational programs are usually accredited by the state. The institution may offer special education, basic classes in a range of subjects, and even college prep classes. Some residents work toward passing the GED (General Education Development test), which grants the equivalent of a high school diploma. Residents may have the opportunity to work with a tutor or mentor. Many institutions also offer vocational programs such as carpentry, automobile repair, and training in electrical work.

Schooling conditions are often substandard, however, especially in large training schools. Teachers must provide instruction to teens of various ages and levels of education. Only about three out of four offenders in residential placement were enrolled in school before being taken into custody. Many have learning disabilities or a history of disciplinary problems. Institutions often lack basic resources, such as computers, textbooks, and equipment for vocational facilities.

Facilities also offer a variety of rehabilitative and mental health services. Residents may participate in programs such as substance abuse counseling, anger management counseling, group therapy sessions, general life skills classes, and individual as well as family therapy. Some facilities target specific types of offenders with programs such as antigang efforts or sex offender treatment. Although some facilities do offer this broad range of resources, others have been criticized for providing inadequate mental health services.

Recreational activities may include sports, movies and television, and field trips. Religious services are offered at many institutions. Some facilities allow—or require—residents to pursue volunteer activities, such as helping out in a local animal shelter or working with a civic organization.

Security and Discipline

Security measures are tightest at public facilities, especially large training schools, and are most lenient at smaller, private facilities. Interestingly, according to a 2010 DOJ study, offenders in unlocked units were much more likely to get along well with facility staff members than those in locked units.

Offenders are disciplined for a range of misconduct, from making threats or getting into fights to possessing contraband or assaulting staff. Punishments may be meted out to an entire group of misbehavers or to individuals. Typical punishments include being locked in one's room, getting extra chores, or losing television privileges. Isolation in solitary confinement is also common. In the DOJ study, more than 10 percent of the offenders placed in solitary confinement claimed they had been held there for longer than twenty-four hours, a practice recommended only in rare circumstances. In addition, staff members may use pepper spray and restraints, such as handcuffs or a restraint chair, but this is justified only when there is absolutely no other way of dealing with an out-of-control offender.

Residential facilities generally provide basic health care to residents. They also screen offenders for substance abuse problems, asking questions about drug use as well as conducting drug tests. Most facilities evaluate the mental health of incoming residents. Almost all facilities evaluate new residents for suicide risk upon their arrival.

Safety

Any offender, as well as his or her family, is bound to worry about whether a teenager given a residential placement will be in a safe environment. There are periodic reports in the media about abuse and brutality in juvenile detention facilities—is the subject overhyped or is the danger real? Sadly, such stories highlight the vulnerability of young offenders who may be taken far from their families and put in a setting where they have very little control over their circumstances.

Many of the offenders in residential facilities are among the most violent and chronic offenders, but nonviolent offenders are also sent to residential facilities. Often, nonviolent offenders are housed in units with violent offenders who are at least three years older than them. This places the younger youth in potential jeopardy and puts him or her in close proximity to a serious offender—not a favorable factor for rehabilitation. Despite high security, fights may break out, especially in facilities where many residents are involved in gangs. Offenders sometimes manage to smuggle in contraband, such as weapons or drugs. Overcrowding worsens the safety and security failings.

For some residents, mistreatment comes not from peers but from staff members. There have been numerous instances of staff being charged with excessive use of isolation or restraints. Even more shocking are cases of sexual abuse by facility staff members. According to a 2010 DOJ report, one in ten offenders in confinement reported being sexually victimized by a staff member.

Precise rates of abuse and mistreatment can be hard to measure. Residential facilities have a grievance procedure to address complaints against staff, but victims are often unwilling to come forward. Youth in residential facilities often feel that the system is prejudiced against them. They may think that they will not be believed or that they will receive retaliation, rather than justice, for speaking out.

Ten Great Questions to Ask a Legal Expert

1 What is the upper age limit of juvenile court jurisdiction in my state?

2 Is it legal in my state for the police to interrogate juveniles without a lawyer or other adult present?

3 After an offender is taken into custody, what is the maximum amount of time he or she will have to wait before a detention hearing according to state law?

4 What are the laws and penalties for status offenses in my state?

5 Where is the juvenile court in my county or city, and who is the judge?

6 What are the state laws for transferring a juvenile offender to adult criminal court?

7 What types of offenses are most likely to result in a penalty of commitment to a detention facility?

(Ten Great Questions to Ask a Legal Expert— *continued*)

8 What types of detention facilities are operated in my state?

9 Do detention facilities in my state have problems such as overcrowding or underfunding?

10 What is the process for expunging a juvenile record in my state?

CHAPTER five

WHAT HAPPENS AFTER LEAVING JUVENILE DETENTION?

After leaving a residential facility, it's natural for any teenager to feel a great sense of relief at being free. Actually, though, involvement in the juvenile justice system continues even after release from confinement. The offender still must conform to conditions of aftercare, a period of supervision following reentry into the community. Aftercare is the juvenile justice equivalent of parole, although the system places a greater emphasis than the criminal justice system on rehabilitation.

A newly free offender has to readjust to living at home and returning to regular school, work, and social activities. It is important that he or she does not fall back into the same pattern of behavior that led to involvement in the juvenile justice system. A juvenile judge is likely to be harsher on repeat offenders. Aftercare is an essential measure in reducing the likelihood of recidivism. For some types of residential placement, such as boot camp and group homes, positive results have been linked to effective aftercare, rather than to the specific focus of the program.

Aftercare

An offender's period of aftercare is generally overseen by an aftercare worker, usually associated with probation or corrections departments. The conditions for aftercare are similar to probation monitoring—there may be a curfew, drug and alcohol screening, electronic surveillance, community service requirements, check-ins with the officer, and other requirements depending on the individual case. Serious offenders are more likely to be intensely monitored than lesser offenders. Often, the young person begins with a high level of supervision that gives way to greater independence as he or she demonstrates good progress.

In addition to imposing restraints, effective aftercare programs also provide services to offenders and their families. Some of these are intervention measures—they aim to prevent juvenile crime by changing the offender's behavior. Examples include life skills instruction and counseling of various types. In some states, youth might attend day treatment programs during the transition back home. Other possible services include vocational or employment training programs.

Ideally, preliminary aftercare planning begins with the judge's disposition and continues throughout the offender's

Students paint a mural at the Northwest Regional Learning Center in Everett, Washington, a school where juvenile offenders on probation or aftercare can work toward a high school diploma.

period of confinement. When the offender is released, the after-care worker is aware of his or her progress and needs. He or she may help the youth deal with practical issues, such as transferring school records and making sure that a parent or guardian is ready for the individual's return. Some jurisdictions have instituted specialized reentry courts that plan and monitor the offender's transition.

In reality, however, many offenders receive minimal aftercare attention. Probation and corrections officers tend to have large caseloads. Different agencies often fail to coordinate efforts in tracking an offender's progress and designing an aftercare plan. The system often lacks the resources to put into action a personalized aftercare plan that will optimally address the youth's needs.

Your Juvenile Record

Many teens who have been through the juvenile justice system assume that their records are sealed when they turn eighteen years old. This is not always true. A juvenile record can have implications far into adulthood, depending on state law.

In order to have a juvenile court record cleared, an individual may have to file an expungement motion in court. Technically, "expungement" means that records are completely destroyed, but they may merely be sealed. Eligibility for expungement varies between states and even between counties within states. Certain violent or habitual offenders may be denied expungement. Even after expungement, some government agencies may be able to access the records.

In some cases, former offenders do not learn about their lasting juvenile record until it has already caused negative consequences. Some information on juvenile offenses may be a matter of public record, available to employers and anyone else who might be interested. A juvenile record can affect eligibility for some government programs, such as college financial aid. In some cases, juvenile offenses legally do not have to be disclosed when a former offender is asked questions about his or her background. Sometimes, though, such as in applying to the military, a juvenile court record is considered as a factor for eligibility.

A student officially graduates from high school at the Metro Regional Youth Detention Center in Atlanta, Georgia—an encouraging success story for the juvenile justice system.

The Overall Effectiveness of Juvenile Detention

The juvenile justice system aims to rehabilitate offenders, using various methods to turn them away from bad behavior. But how well does it work? How likely is it that an offender who undergoes residential placement and aftercare will be set straight by the juvenile justice system?

The usual means of examining effectiveness is the recidivism rate—whether the offender is rearrested, either as a juvenile or later as an adult. Unfortunately, though, recidivism is hard to measure, and much of the information collected relies on different criteria. A DOJ report avoids the issue, stating that there is no national recidivism rate because "such a rate would not have much meaning since juvenile justice systems vary so much across states." Nevertheless, individual states or institutions can measure rates of improvement or decline by comparing newly collected data to older records.

Partial information on recidivism rates is still revealing. Three states, for example, tracked the rate of arrest for offenders within a year of release and found a recidivism rate of 55 percent. Eight states tracked rates of reconviction within a year of release, either in the criminal or juvenile justice system, and reported a recidivism rate of 33 percent. These are alarmingly high statistics.

The failings of the juvenile justice system run deeper than the numbers. As seen earlier, residential facilities fail to meet the educational and treatment needs of many offenders. Facilities tend to be overcrowded and pinched for resources. Too many offenders are abused or mistreated in confinement. Minority youth are disproportionately represented in the juvenile justice system. In addition, the system does not address the needs of specific groups within the system. Gay and lesbian offenders, for example, are more likely to be harassed or assaulted. Young people who are pregnant or parenting present special challenges to the system.

What's more, there has been evidence that detention and residential placement is linked to higher rates of recidivism. Part of this is the phenomenon of peer deviancy training. Essentially, exposure to troublemakers can really rub off on better behaved young people. When at-risk teenagers are brought together as a group, such as in detention or residential facilities, it tends to intensify bad behavior.

Finally, there is the matter of the high cost of juvenile confinement. It might seem wrong to try to put a price limit on such an important issue that can determine the futures of many young people. But despite the money being spent on juvenile confinement, it is a flawed practice that fails many young people. Many experts agree that policy makers should pursue reform measures that both make financial sense and better meet the needs of young offenders.

Toward Reform

It is easy to list the shortcomings of the juvenile justice system and residential facilities, but it is much more difficult to put new ideas into practice. Part of this dilemma is ideological. There are many different proposals for reform, many of them untested. Before a program is applied on a large scale, its effectiveness must be proven. Moving from theory to practice to the large-scale carrying out of a plan is a long process that can be derailed at any stage along the way. There are also practical difficulties. Instituting large-scale reform can be a complex and expensive undertaking. In addition, policy makers have political concerns.

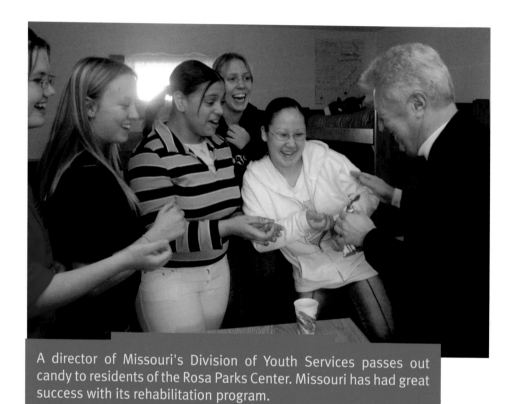

A director of Missouri's Division of Youth Services passes out candy to residents of the Rosa Parks Center. Missouri has had great success with its rehabilitation program.

Despite evidence that committing juvenile offenders to residential facilities does not improve public safety or reduce recidivism, no politician wants to be accused of being "soft on crime" and letting offenders off lightly.

Nonetheless, there is broad agreement on a number of points. The juvenile justice system should reorient itself back toward rehabilitation rather than punishment. The overall number of offenders held in detention and residential facilities should be reduced. In particular, nonviolent offenders should be given alternative dispositions to confinement. Community-based programs should be emphasized as an alternative.

Conditions should be improved for offenders who are placed in residential facilities. The reasons for the lopsided numbers of minority offenders in the system should be examined and the inequalities should be addressed.

It might seem that the sweeping reforms necessary to incorporate all of these proposals would ultimately be impractical and expensive. The juvenile justice system in one state, however, has emerged as a success story and an example studied by juvenile justice systems across the country. The Missouri model emphasizes early intervention for offenders, providing a variety of community services. When possible, the court encourages a strong family and community support system, rather than sending young people away. Residential facilities are small, with fewer than fifty residents in the largest, and create a homelike atmosphere. Offenders work with the same staff members throughout their involvement in the system. For policy makers, the surest indicator of success is Missouri's low recidivism rate: in 2009, it was under 15 percent for the year following offenders' release. The Missouri model is not guaranteed to work in every state, but it does provide an encouraging instance of effective reform that genuinely helps the young people who are drawn into the juvenile justice system.

Glossary

adjudication The process in which a judge rules on whether or not a juvenile has committed a delinquent act.

adversarial Involving or characterized by conflict or opposition.

bail A sum of money deposited to secure an accused person's temporary release from custody and to guarantee that person's appearance in court at a later date. If the person fails to appear in court on the date set, the money is forfeited.

chronic Subject to a pattern of behavior for a long time; for offenders, having a record of numerous arrests or convictions.

community service Work performed by offenders as part of their sentence.

contraband Smuggled goods.

culpability Deserved blame or punishment for a wrongdoing.

custody Legal restraint or detention; also, guardianship, such as in a child custody case.

daunting Intimidating or discouraging.

delinquency The violation of a law by a juvenile.

deterrence The act of preventing or discouraging someone from doing something; a theory that criminal laws are passed with well-defined punishments to discourage individual criminal defendants from becoming repeat offenders and to discourage others from engaging in similar criminal activity.

discretion The power of a judge or other official to make judgments based on principles of law and fairness.

disposition The final determination in a case; the juvenile justice equivalent of a court sentence.

diversion A type of informal probation in which a case is not formally processed by the juvenile court.

evidence Data presented in court in proof of facts in a case.

expungement The act of erasing or canceling out.

incarceration Imprisonment, confinement, or detention.

interrogate To ask questions of someone very thoroughly, often in an aggressive or threatening manner, especially as part of a formal investigation, for example, in a police station or courtroom.

intervention Interference; having come between two people or things.

jurisdiction The right or power to administer justice.

juvenile A young person at or beneath the age of juvenile court jurisdiction.

larceny The unlawful taking of personal property with the intention of keeping it permanently from the rightful owner.

mete out To give out by measure; to dispense or allot justice, a punishment, or harsh treatment.

minor A person who is not legally adult; someone younger than the legal age of adulthood.

offender One who has committed an illegal act.

penalty A punishment imposed for breaking a rule or law.

probable cause A reasonable ground for supposing that a charge is well-founded.

probation The act of suspending an offender's sentence and allowing him or her to go free subject to certain conditions.

ramification An usually unintended consequence of an action, decision, or judgment that may complicate a situation or make the desired result more difficult to achieve.

recidivism The tendency to relapse to a previous pattern of behavior, especially crime.

rehabilitation The restoration of an offender to a law-abiding individual.

restitution Money or services given in compensation of loss or injury.

restrictive Tending to limit; acting as a limit or control on something.

sanction A penalty for breaking the law.

status offense Conduct that is illegal for a juvenile but non-criminal for an adult.

waiver The act of relinquishing a right, claim, or privilege.

Canadian Bar Association (CBA)

500 - 865 Carling Avenue

Ottawa, ON K1S 5S8

Canada

Web site: http://www.cba.org

This organization is made up of members of Canada's legal
  profession.

Canadian Institute for the Administration of Justice (CIAJ)

Faculty of Law

University of Montreal

Pavilion Maximilien-Caron

3101 Chemin de la Tour, Room 3421

P.O. Box 6128, Station Centre Ville

Montreal, QC H3C 3J7

Canada

(514) 343-6157

Web site: http://www.ciaj-icaj.ca

CIAJ is a nonprofit organization dedicated to improving the
  quality of justice for all Canadians.

Coalition for Juvenile Justice (CJJ)

1710 Rhode Island Avenue NW, 10th Floor

Washington, DC 20036

(202) 467-0864

Web site: http://www.juvjustice.org

CJJ is a national nonprofit association that represents fifty-six governor-appointed advisory groups supporting the juvenile court system in the United States, its territories, and the District of Columbia.

Juvenile Law Center (JLC)

1315 Walnut Street, 4th Floor

Philadelphia, PA 19107

(215) 625-0551

Web site: http://www.jlc.org

This nonprofit legal service is devoted to advancing the rights and well-being of children in jeopardy.

National Center for Juvenile Justice (NCJJ)

3700 South Water Street, Suite 200

Pittsburgh, Pa 15203

(412) 227-6950

Web site: http://www.ncjj.org

A division of the National Council of Juvenile and Family Court Judges, NCJJ aims to provide effective justice for children and their families through research and technical assistance.

National Juvenile Defender Center (NJDC)

1350 Connecticut Avenue NW, Suite 304

Washington, DC 20036

(202) 452-0010

Web site: http://njdc.info

NJDC is dedicated to improving the quality and access of legal
counsel available to youths in court.

Office of Juvenile Justice and Delinquency Prevention (OJJDP)
810 Seventh Street NW
Washington, DC 20531
(202) 307–5911
Web site: http://www.ojjdp.gov
Part of the U.S. Department of Justice, OJJDP provides
national leadership, coordination, and resources to prevent
and respond to juvenile delinquency and victimization.

Web Sites

Due to the changing nature of Internet links, Rosen Publishing
has developed an online list of Web sites related to the subject
of this book. This site is updated regularly. Please use this link
to access the list:

http://www.rosenlinks.com/faq/jdet

For Further Reading

Chura, David. *I Don't Wish Nobody to Have a Life Like Mine: Tales of Kids in Adult Lockup.* Boston, MA: Beacon Press, 2010.

Finley, Laura L. *Juvenile Justice.* Westport, CT: Greenwood Press, 2007.

Gold, Susan Dudley. *In Re Gault: Do Minors Have the Same Rights as Adults?* New York, NY: Benchmark Books, 2007.

Goodman, Shawn. *Something Like Hope.* New York, NY: Delacorte Books for Young Readers, 2010.

Grimming, Rob, and Debbie J. Goodman. *Juvenile Justice: A Collection of True-Crime Cases.* Upper Saddle River, NJ: Pearson Education, 2008.

Hamilton, Jill. *Juvenile Crime: Social Issues Firsthand.* San Diego, CA: Greenhaven Press, 2009.

Humes, Edward. *No Matter How Loud I Shout: A Year in the Life of Juvenile Court.* New York, NY: Simon and Schuster, 1997.

Jacobs, Thomas A. *Teens Take It to Court: Young People Who Challenged the Law—and Changed Your Life.* Minneapolis, MN: Free Spirit Publishing, 2006.

Jacobs, Thomas A. *What Are My Rights? Ninety-Five Questions and Answers About Teens and the Law.* Minneapolis, MN: Free Spirit Publishing, 2006.

Leverich, Jean. *Juvenile Justice: Issues on Trial.* San Diego, CA: Greenhaven Press, 2009.

Liss, Steve. *No Place for Children: Voices from Juvenile Detention.* Austin, TX: University of Texas Press, 2005.

Marcovitz, Hal. *Gangs.* Edina, MN: ABDO Publishing, 2010.

Merino, Noel, ed. *Juvenile Crime* (Introducing Issues with Opposing Viewpoints). Farmington Hills, MI: Greenhaven Press, 2010.

Myers, Walter Dean. *Lockdown.* New York, NY: Amistad, 2010.

Nurse, Anne M. *Locked Up, Locked Out: Young Men in the Juvenile Justice System.* Nashville, TN: Vanderbilt University Press, 2010.

Salzman, Mark. *True Notebooks: A Writer's Year at Juvenile Hall.* New York, NY: Vintage Books, 2004.

Seventeen. Seventeen Real Girls, Real-Life Stories: True Crime. New York, NY: Hearst Books, 2007.

Smith, Roger. *Youth in Prison.* Broomall, PA: Mason Crest Publishers, 2006.

Truly, Traci. *Teen Rights (and Responsibilities): A Legal Guide for Teens and the Adults in Their Lives.* Naperville, IL: Sphinx Publications, 2005.

Williams, Heidi. *Juvenile Crime: Issues That Concern You.* Farmington Hills, MI: Greenhaven Press, 2010.

Index

About the Author

Corona Brezina is an author who has written numerous books for young adults, some of which have focused on social and legal issues concerning teens, including *Careers in the Juvenile Justice System* and *Deadly School and Campus Violence*. She lives in Chicago, Illinois.

Photo Credits

Cover © www.istockphoto.com/Windzepher; p. 6 © MIKE BROWN/ The Commercial Appeal/Landov; p. 9 Photodisc/Thinkstock.com; p. 11 Linda Davidson/The Washington Post/Getty Images; p. 18 www.ojjdp.gov; p. 20 © Sacramento Bee/ZUMApress.com; p. 23 © Marlin Levison /Star Tribune/ZUMA Press; p. 26 CHUCK KENNEDY/KRT/Newscom; p. 28 © Larry Kolvoord/The Image Works; p. 32 © Journal Courier/The Image Works; p. 35 © Augusta Chronicle/ZUMAPRESS.com; pp. 37, 47, 49, 52 © AP Images; p.39 Antonio Perez/Chicago Tribune/MCT via Getty Images.

Editor: Kathy Kuhtz Campbell; Photo Researcher: Amy Feinberg